HA... TAKES THE LEAD

R J Whittaker

Also by R J Whittaker

Jasmine Moves In
Pom Pom The Great
Pom Pom Moves House
Pom Pom Starts School
Pom Pom The Pirate
Pom Pom the Brave
Pom Pom Helps Out

For Saffron – who will one day be even more successful than Hannah

One

I think I'm going to throw up in front of the whole drama club. We're waiting for the cast list to be announced, and I can hardly bear it. Even the cool girls sitting there snapping their gum really want to hear who's been chosen. Of course, they'd rather die than show they're interested, but this play is more important to me than anything else in the world, and I don't care who knows it.

I've always wanted to be an actor, but I never get any good parts. I was the Christmas Star in our year five nativity play, but I don't think that really counts. My costume was made of tinsel-covered coat hangers, which poked into my arms and legs whenever I moved, and I had to wave dramatically towards the stable each time a group of shepherds or wise men appeared. Mum said it was a start, but Dad said I reminded him of a piece of sparkly seaweed.

I'm going to be a proper actor when I grow up - a really famous one. I'll probably move to Hollywood and hang out with all the stars – the real stars, I mean, not just the ones covered in tinsel and coat hangers. Until then, I need to get as much acting experience as possible, and this school play is a great opportunity.

Our high school drama club meets after school each week and puts on a show each year. Last year they did *Grease*, which means we won't be doing a musical this year. I'm really pleased about that because I can't sing. I'm not being modest when I say that. I really can't sing a note. My year five music teacher offered me a chocolate bar if I'd only pretend to sing at our end of term concert, because someone from the Department of Education was coming to inspect her work. It was really nice chocolate, all the way from Switzerland, and I gave it to my brother Scott in exchange for a week's dishwasher duty.

We had our auditions last week, and I have no idea why it's taken Miss Ryner so long to cast the parts. We're doing *Charlie and the Chocolate Factory*, and the girls in the art club have already started painting the scenery. They've made a gorgeous backdrop of a chocolate river, and now they're working on a plastic tube for Augustus Gloop.

I have absolutely no chance of a lead role, but I really want a speaking part, however small. I'd love to be Veruca Salt, the spoiled rich girl, but everyone knows Stephanie Rider will get that part. She has the loudest voice of anyone I know – and the poshest. Even I have to admit she'll be perfect.

I'm secretly hoping to be one of Charlie's grandmothers. They have lots of funny lines, and I love making people laugh. My brother Scott, who thinks he's all that, told me I'll definitely be an Oompa Loompa because I'm so small, but I said I'd rather not be in the play at all than dress up as a stupid Oompa Loompa.

Mum overheard and said I won't get very far as an actor if that's my attitude. Actors have to take any part they can get for years and years, until they get their big break. I know she's right, but when you've always been the smallest person in your year and your nickname is *Fun Size*, it's embarrassing to have to paint your face orange and dance around the stage, with everyone laughing at you instead of with you.

The classroom door opens, and Miss Ryner comes in. I let out a gasp of excitement and my best friend Ashleigh gives my hand a sympathetic squeeze. She's only here for moral support, because she says she'd rather die than act in a play. If I get a part, she's promised to help me with my lines and wait for me during rehearsals so we can walk home together as usual.

Miss Ryner gives us a cheerful smile and waves a sheet of paper. 'Good afternoon, girls.'

I beam back at her. 'Good afternoon!' I must have spoken more loudly than I intended because everyone laughs, including Miss Ryner.

'Nice to see so much enthusiasm, Hannah,' she says, perching herself on the edge of a desk. 'Now, I know you're all dying to find out who's playing the main parts, so I won't keep you waiting. I just want to say one thing first. There are only a few main characters in any production, so most people will have supporting roles. I'd like you to remember that every single part is important. Without the supporting cast the play would collapse entirely. Do you all agree?'

We nod, but I'd like to see Miss Ryner play a tinsel-covered star when what she really wanted was to be Mary, or at least a shepherd. Even a lamb would have been better than nothing.

Miss Ryner glances down at her list. 'After much thought, Mr Markson and I have cast the main parts as follows: Grandpa Joe – Minnie Heywood, Veruca Salt – Stephanie Rider, Augustus Gloop – Olivia O'Donnell ...'

Most people laugh when she says this. Olivia is very tall and thin, with long, blonde hair. She'll have to wear lots of padding, but she's in the top group for German, so she'll probably get the accent right.

Miss Ryner reads through the list of main characters without calling my name. Of course, she doesn't. I tell myself that I'm totally not disappointed because I never expected her to choose me. I didn't really want a part in her stupid play anyway.

She puts the list back in her bag. 'If your name wasn't called, you'll be an Oompa Loompa.'

I turn away to hide my disappointment. I knew I wouldn't get a main part, but I'd desperately hoped for something small. For once in his life, I wanted to see Scott lost for words. I wanted Mum to beam with pride and Dad to say something teasing and stupid, to hide the fact he was proud of me. Now, I have to go home and tell everyone I'm an Oompa Loompa and put up with Scott imitating me and doing squeaky voices for the next few months. Sometimes, I *hate* being so small and skinny. They'd never have cast Stephanie Rider as an Oompa Loompa.

'Never mind,' whispers Ashleigh. 'There's always next year.'

I just nod because I don't trust myself to speak.

Natasha Roberts is waving frantically at Miss Ryner. 'You didn't mention Charlie! Who's going to play Charlie?'

'I wondered when someone was going to ask,' says Miss Ryner. 'It was a very tough decision, but one person definitely stood out from the rest. The part of Charlie will be played by Hannah Davies.'

No one speaks for a moment. I'm busy looking around the room for this Hannah person when it hits me. Miss Ryner means me! I'm going to play Charlie Bucket. I'm not a stupid Oompa Loompa, after all. I'm Charlie, the star of the whole show!

Ashleigh gives me a huge grin. 'Way to go Hannah!'

I grab her hand. 'Did you hear that, Ash? I'm the star! I'm the most important person in the whole play. This is so awesome. I just *knew* I'd done a brilliant audition.'

She pulls her hand away, and I look at her in surprise. 'Are you alright?'

She gives me a tight smile. 'Yeah, it's amazing. Congratulations.'

Everyone gathers around, slapping me on the back and congratulating me. From the looks on their faces, I can tell they're surprised I was chosen. I don' really blame them. Right now, I'm probably the most surprised person in the entire room.

'I'll catch up with you tomorrow, Hannah,' says Miss Ryner as she turns to leave. 'Rehearsals start on Friday, so you'd better take your script now.'

She hands me a bundle of papers, and I look around for Ashleigh. She and I are supposed to be walking home together, but she seems to have disappeared. I pick up my script and make for the door. She's probably gone downstairs to collect her books from her locker.

I set off to find her, feeling a bounce in my feet each time I take a step. I see her waiting by the lockers and finish the flight of stairs at a run, launching myself off the last four steps like Buzz Lightyear.

I can't believe this! I've finally made it! I smile a smile so huge it hurts my ears, but I don't care. Sometimes, I *love* being small and skinny!

Two

My moment of glory lasts for about five minutes. I'm longing to tell my family the news, so I walk home as quickly as possible. As I open the front door, Scott appears from the kitchen, clutching a half-eaten fluffernutter sandwich.

I shoot him a suspicious look. 'Where did you find the marshmallow fluff?'

'On the top shelf behind the laundry powder,' he says through a mouthful of bread. 'Exactly where I'd expect someone like you to hide it. There was half a jar left – just enough for one Scott-sized sandwich.'

I thought I'd hidden the jar where he'd wouldn't find it this time. Peanut butter and marshmallow sandwiches are my absolute favourite, but Mum hardly ever buys the marshmallow fluff. When she does, I usually try to hide it somewhere Scott won't think to look, but he always does.

He takes another huge bite. 'I don't know why you're making so much fuss, anyway. Oompa Loompas don't eat fluffernutters.'

This takes my mind right off the subject of sandwiches, and I give him a huge, triumphant grin. 'No, they don't, but Charlie Bucket does!'

Scott doesn't stop chewing. 'No, he doesn't. He eats cabbage soup.'

I kick myself for allowing him to catch me out. This should have been a really big moment for me. It was my one chance to completely shut him up.

I try again. 'Maybe he does to begin with, but when he goes to the chocolate factory there's probably marshmallow fluff everywhere.'

'Whatever.' He starts to walk towards the stairs.

I run after him and grab his arm, but he shakes me off. I take a deep breath. 'You haven't heard my news yet. I'm Charlie Bucket!'

'Ok,' he says.

'In the play, I mean. I'm the star of the whole play,' I explain.

He shrugs. 'If you say so.'

He wanders off, and a moment later I hear loud music blaring from his room.

So, that didn't quite go to plan. Sometimes, older brothers really suck. Mum and Dad are much more satisfactory when I tell them the news. Dad gives me a high five, and Mum actually cries as she hugs me.

I push her away. 'Stop it, Mum! You're embarrassing me.'

She gulps and wipes her eyes. 'I'm sorry, Hannah. I'm just so proud of you. We'll all be in the audience to cheer you on – Gran and Grandad and Aunty Jen.'

This is actually quite a scary thought. I love my grandparents to bits, but Gran is very deaf and very loud. She always forgets to turn on her hearing aid, so she just shouts a lot instead. It's even worse when she does turn it on. It whistles really loudly and makes everyone around her jump. The thought of her switching it on in the middle of the play and everyone turning to stare makes me hot with embarrassment. Perhaps I'll hide her hearing aid with the marshmallow fluff before we leave the house.

Aunty Jen will be great, of course. She's Mum's sister, and she's a lot of fun. She also gives the very best birthday presents. Last year, she took me to Sydney for the night. We sailed around the harbour and went to the Opera House in the evening. It was the best birthday ever. Aunty Jen is nothing like Mum. She never worries about anything, and she's always laughing. Mum says Aunty Jen would worry all right if she had children of her own, but Aunty Jen says Scott and I are enough for any family, and she'd rather be an aunt than a mother any day.

I call Ashleigh after dinner. Her mum answers and tells me that Ashleigh has gone out with her dad for ice cream, and she'll see me tomorrow at school. It's weird that Ashleigh didn't invite me too. We always do everything together.

I don't see her on the way to school the next day, which is a surprise. We usually meet at the corner of the road and walk down the hill together, past our old primary school and on to Hanfield High. It doesn't seem possible that we were in year six only last summer. It feels as though we've been in high school for ages, and the primary kids playing and shouting in the playground seem really small.

I still haven't seen Ashleigh by morning break, so I set off to look for her. Miss Ryner pops out of her classroom as I walk past. 'Have you had a chance to look at your script yet, Hannah?'

I nod proudly. I spent ages reading my script last night, and I've already memorised the first scene.

Miss Ryner's face lights up when I tell her this.

'That's great!' she says. 'To tell you the truth, I've been a little worried about giving such a large part to a year seven girl. It's an awful lot to learn while you're still busy settling into high school, and we mustn't let your schoolwork suffer. If you think it's going to be too much for you, now's the time to tell me. No one will blame you, and we can always cast an older girl in the part.'

I clutch at her arm in horror. 'Don't take it away from me, Miss Ryner! I can do it. Honestly, I can. I promise I'll work really, really hard.'

She laughs. 'I'm not taking the part away from you. I just don't want you killing yourself over it. I'll see you on Friday for our first rehearsal.'

The bell rings, and I shoot off to my maths lesson as quickly as possible. Mr Chase always takes the roll as soon as he arrives, and he dishes out detentions like confetti if anyone's even a minute late. I throw myself into the seat next to Ashleigh just half a second before he walks in.

'There you are!' I whisper. 'I've been looking for you everywhere. I called your house last night, but your Mum said you were out.'

'I went out with Dad,' she says quietly.

I open my maths book. 'I know you did. Why didn't you invite me too? I could have told him all about the play.'

She doesn't seem to hear me. Mr Chase waves for quiet, looking crosser than ever. 'That's enough now, girls!' he barks. 'I want absolute silence for the roll call.'

He glares around the room, and no one dares to move as he calls out our names. When he gets to *Davies*, he stops and stares at me over the rim of his thick, black glasses. 'Hannah Davies? Miss Ryner tells me you have the leading role in this year's play.'

That's right, sir,' I say with a huge grin. It's nice of him to congratulate me. Perhaps he isn't so bad, after all.

He gives me a stern look. 'Well, I'd like you to remember that your schoolwork comes first. Your maths is very shaky at the best of times. If it gets any worse as a result of this play, you may find yourself shaking all the way down to level two next year.'

I stare down at my desk, trying to ignore him but feeling my face turn scarlet. I hear a couple of girls behind me snicker. I look at Ashleigh for sympathy and am shocked to see her grinning at Macy Phillips. Ashleigh and I never laugh at one other. We stick together, come what may.

That's how we met all the way back in year one, when Matt Rogers was making fun of Ashleigh for having red hair. I saw her crying in the sandpit one day, so I went over and karate-kicked him for her. She was waiting for me when I came out of the Principal's office with a letter for Mum, and we've been best friends ever since. I can't believe she's laughing at me now.

The maths lesson crawls past, and I hardly listen to what Mr Chase is teaching us. It doesn't matter, anyway. I can just copy off Ashleigh. She never minds. She's really good at maths and doesn't have to try at all. I find French easy, so I help her with that. That's the way it's always worked for us – helping each other, sticking together.

Mr Chase drones to a stop at last and scribbles something on the white board. 'I want that handed in by Friday,' he tells us. 'No excuses, no extensions. Is that clearly understood?'

I think he might be looking at me when he says this, but I ignore him. Ashleigh will have to tell me what we're supposed to be doing because I haven't followed any of today's lesson. My head has been completely full of chocolate rivers and sugar flowers. I wonder whether they'll let us eat the candy during the actual performance.

Mr Chase gathers his papers together and leaves the room. I turn to ask Ashleigh for a look at her notes, but she's gone. I shoot out of the classroom, but all I can see is her back as she walks down the corridor with Macy. Their heads are close together, and they're giggling about something. It had better not be me.

Three

The rest of the week flies by, and I only remember my stupid maths assignment on Thursday afternoon. When I ask Ashleigh about it, she explains what we're supposed to do but says she isn't free to do our homework together that evening.

'Are you upset about me being Charlie?' I ask directly.

She frowns. 'Of course not, but you'll be pretty busy this term, and I'm busy with stuff too.'

'Like what?' I ask.

'You aren't the only person who has a life,' she says, closing her book. 'As a matter of fact, I'm learning to ride.'

I feel a twinge of jealousy when she says this. She and I have often asked for riding lessons, but our parents have always said they're out of the question. We'll definitely have to learn to ride sometime because we plan to buy a huge ranch up in Queensland when we're older. We're going to keep lots of horses, and I'll go there to rest between making movies.

'Hey, shall I check if I can come too?' I ask. 'If your mum's letting you learn to ride, I bet mine would say yes as well.'

Ashleigh's face turns red. 'Sorry, Hannah, but that wouldn't work. I'm going riding with Macy.'

'Macy?' I ask, trying not to let a note of jealousy creep into my voice. 'I didn't know you were friends with Macy.'

She shrugs. 'Well, I am. She keeps her own horse in the field behind her house, and her dad's going to teach me to ride in the evenings. It'll be really fun.'

I give her a cool stare. 'I don't expect I'd be able to, even if I wanted to. The play's going to take up all my spare time.'

'That's what I thought,' she agrees. 'Sorry, Hannah.'

She does actually sound quite sorry, but I refuse to meet her halfway. I can't believe she's been sneaky enough to arrange riding lessons behind my back.

'Don't be sorry,' I say coldly. 'Miss Ryner probably wouldn't let me ride anyway. She can't risk me falling and breaking my leg. I'm far too important. They couldn't do the play without Charlie Bucket.'

Ashleigh's face freezes. 'Is that right?' she asks and walks away without another word.

I rush through my maths assignment as quickly as possible and spend the rest of the evening learning my lines. I'm really nervous about our first rehearsal. I've memorised the first three scenes, but I'm still scared I'll forget the words when other people are around. Scott offers to help me with my lines, which surprises me a bit, but he changes the words around just to confuse me, and I end up throwing the script at him and storming out.

When I walk into the hall the following afternoon, Miss Ryner introduces me to the girls I haven't already met. I already know Grandpa Joe and Mrs Bucket from the swim team, but most of the others are in year ten, and they don't usually mix with year sevens. They're really nice to me, and I overhear some of them saying how cute I am, and that I must be a really good actor if I'm only in year seven, which makes me feel a lot more confident.

The only bad moment is when Miss Ryner brings Rose Simms over to talk to me. Rose only moved to our town this year, just in time to start at Hanfield High, and I don't really like her. She hardly says a word to anyone, and Ashleigh and I think she's a bit of a snob. She looks as though she thinks she's better than everyone else, and she never seems to join in with anything. I wonder why she's here today.

'Hannah, I expect you already know Rose,' says Miss Ryner. You're both in year seven. She's going to be your understudy for the part of Charlie.'

Just for once, I'm lost for words. '*Understudy?*' I ask blankly.

'It's someone who learns your part and goes on instead of you if there's any problem,' explains Miss Ryner.

I know exactly what an understudy is – I just didn't expect to have one. It's all so stupid. I didn't have an understudy when I was a Christmas star. There was no one waiting around in the wings ready to dress up in my coat hangers and tinsel in an emergency and point gracefully towards the stable.

'I don't really think I need an understudy, Miss Ryner,' I tell her cheerfully. 'There's no point, and it would just be wasting Rose's time.'

I add this to show I'm only thinking of Rose and all her wasted hours watching the rehearsals. I don't add that she's the last person I'd ever want as my understudy.

Miss Ryner gives me rather an odd look. 'I think Mr Markson and I will be the best judges of that. We always have understudies for our main parts, and it's saved us several times in past productions. Rose will be coming to all the rehearsals, and you can get together and practise your scenes at other times. It will be nice for you to have someone your own age to chat to while we're rehearsing the scenes that don't involve you.'

I can tell there's no point arguing, but I refuse to sit and talk to Rose Simms during every rehearsal.

As for practising lines with her, she can just forget it.

'Ok,' I say at last, nodding at Rose because Miss Ryner is still watching me.

Rose doesn't say anything – just looks at me in silence. She's always like that.

We start with the first scene, which goes quite well. At least I don't forget any of my lines. Mr Markson shows me exactly where to stand at each point.

'Never turn your back to the audience, Hannah,' he tells me. 'Even when someone else is speaking, the audience wants to see your face, so they know exactly what you're thinking and how you're reacting. Turn towards them properly each time you speak, so you can throw your voice right to the back of the hall.'

To be honest, I've never had much problem throwing my voice as far as I want to. It comes of growing up with a brother like Scott. I must admit that Dad has a point when he calls me *Foghorn*, and

Mum says that even as a baby, you could hear me bawling halfway down the street when I was tired or hungry. I'm also the only person Gran can hear properly without turning on her hearing aid.

I get even louder when I'm excited or happy, but I can't help it. Teachers are always shushing me and telling me to keep my voice down, but what's the point of whispering when you're excited? Life is too much fun to stay quiet.

'I've been wondering whether we ought to put in a few songs for the main characters, as well as the Oompa Loompas,' Miss Ryner says thoughtfully.

I jump in shock. 'I don't think so!' I almost shout, and she gives me a surprised look.

'Sorry,' I say more quietly, 'but I just don't think we need any more songs. It's a really good play without them.'

'You may be right,' she says. 'We do need to keep the whole thing under an hour and a half. Perhaps we'll wait and see how it goes.'

I breathe a sigh of relief before catching sight of some of the Oompa Loompas grinning at me from the front row of chairs. Most of them are in year seven like me, and we were all in primary school together, so they know what my singing voice is like. I turn away and ignore them. They're only what Miss Ryner calls the 'supporting cast', so I don't see what right they have to laugh at any of the main characters.

We finish the first scene then watch the Oompa Loompas practising one of their dances. I'm *so* glad I don't have to paint my face and do stupid jigs. It's much more fun being the star of the whole thing.

We finish rehearsing at five o'clock, and I bundle everything into my bag in a hurry. Mum says that dinner will be on the table at five thirty every day, and she wants me there. I have to promise to eat properly and make sure I don't get behind on my homework assignments, or she'll have to see Miss Ryner about it. That would be beyond embarrassing, but I know she means it, so I'd better be home on time.

I wave goodbye to the older girls as I leave, and several of them grin back at me. 'Bye, Charlie! See you on Monday.'

This is really great. They must think I'm good if they're already calling me Charlie. I swing my bag confidently onto my shoulder and walk towards the door. As I open it, I'm almost sure I see Ashleigh waiting for me outside the main entrance, and I breathe a sigh of relief. She's obviously seen sense at last. I'm just heading over to meet her when Mr Markson appears behind me.

'I wanted to catch you before you left to say how pleased we are with your performance,' he says. 'We've definitely made the right choice for the lead role. You're going to be a star!'

I grin back at him. 'Thanks, Mr Markson. I'm really enjoying it.'

'That's half the battle,' he says. 'Bye, then, Hannah.'

I turn back to look for Ashleigh, but there's no one there. I guess I must have imagined it.

Four

By the middle of term, things are starting to get really busy. Not only do I have an entire script to learn, but we're also rehearsing three times a week, and I sometimes have separate rehearsals with Miss Ryner. Sadly, Rose always comes to these, but apart from that they're really good, and I love the one-to-one attention.

Rose doesn't say much during rehearsals Unless Miss Ryner asks her to try a scene, she just sits there watching and making notes in her script She must have quite a good memory because she appears to have memorised the entire script already She's actually ok when she acts – a bit quiet perhaps but not too bad. But I really think they've made the right choice in giving the part to me. I'm growing more confident by the day. Everyone seems to think I'm doing really well, and so do I.

On the other hand, I'm starting to feel as though I'm juggling china plates. It's only two plates at first which isn't too bad – in fact, it's quite fun. However as the weeks go by, people keep throwing me extra plates, and I have to keep them all in the air at once If I don't, there'll be the biggest crash ever, and I'll be standing in the corridor, surrounded by broken plates, with everyone staring at me and laughing.

I'm also finding it more and more difficult to sleep each night, and I'm starting to get annoyed by all Mum's fussing. She keeps insisting that I eat regular meals, but there's just so much else to do. Some of the teachers are pretty mean too. You'd think they might want to give the star a break, but they don't seem to agree. Mr Chase even keeps me in at lunchtime one day because I can't get my decimal fractions right. I bet that none of the Hollywood stars can do decimal fractions. They probably have *people* to do those for them.

It's just the same with my French lessons. Hollywood films aren't in French, so the subject isn't a lot of use to me, but Mademoiselle Cartier doesn't see it like that.

'You are ze most inattentive pupil in ze entire class,' she scolds me, and I frown back at her. I'm sick of teachers putting me down in front of the rest of the class, especially when Ashleigh's there. I hardly ever see her to talk to nowadays, but it's still horrible to see her sitting next to Macy, trying not to smile when I get told off.

I grab her arm as she walks past me after our French lesson. 'Why are you being so mean?' I hiss, low enough for Macy not to hear.

Ashleigh shakes off my hand. 'I'm not being anything, Hannah. Don't be stupid.'

'I'm not the one being stupid!' I snap. 'You didn't have to dump me just because I was given the best part in the play. I'd still have made time for you somehow.'

She looks at me as though I'm an alien being. 'Oh, thanks a lot, Hannah. How nice of you to fit me into your timetable.'

I scuff my shoe on the ground. 'I didn't mean it like that, but you must know how busy I've been. You could have fitted around me a bit.'

'Just beautiful!' she says, pushing past me and walking away with Macy.

At least I know where I stand with her now. If I can't give her all my time and attention, she just isn't interested. Well, this play is more important than anything – schoolwork, swimming, even Ashleigh. If she can't accept that, I'm much better off without her.

Anyway, I seem to be making new friends pretty easily. Plenty of people who've never spoken to me before now say hi when they pass me in the corridor, and all the older girls in the play are really nice to me.

A year eight girl comes into our maths class one Monday morning, just as Mr Chase is handing back our assignments. I'm slightly nervous about mine. The assignment wasn't really that difficult, but it was quite complicated and needed much more time than I was able to spare for it. I was really tired by the end, so I just scribbled the last part and hoped for the best. From the look on Mr Chase's face, I can tell that wasn't good enough.

The girl hands him a note, and he quickly scans it then frowns. 'Does it have to be right now, Anna?'

I can't hear what she says, but he shrugs his shoulders and points to me. 'Apparently, you're wanted. Please get back here as quickly as possible. You simply can't afford to miss your maths lessons.'

He waves my assignment at me as he speaks. I can't see the actual grade, but it's covered in red ink, which is always a bad sign. I catch Ashleigh's eye, and she gives me a sympathetic look. I give her a half smile back. I've really missed her helping me out with maths. She finds it so easy, while I absolutely hate it.

'Where's Hannah going, sir?' asks Melanie. She's incredibly nosy and can't bear not knowing everyone's business. In primary school, we called her Pinocchio.

'The photography class is doing the publicity shots for the play,' Mr Chase says crossly.

Ashleigh immediately looks away, but I don't really care. This is so cool. I'm going to have my picture all over the school. I skip out of the class and follow Anna down to the hall.

I have a great time for the next half hour. The photography class is having a competition and the winning pictures will be used as publicity around the school and on the website. Miss Ryner has brought some of the costumes and I dress up as Charlie. She messes up my hair and paints some freckles on my face and everyone crowds around me with their cameras, clicking away. It feels just like being at the Oscars, and I love it.

I pose with a torn open bar of chocolate and an amazed look on my face. Then I pose holding Grandpa Joe's hand and looking scared. All the other characters are here too, but it's obvious everyone really wants to take my picture. They take some pictures of Rose too, which is rather annoying. After all, she's only the stupid understudy.

When the lunch bell rings, Miss Ryner comes over to talk to me. 'Well done, Hannah. I think we'll have some wonderful publicity pictures.'

I smile happily as I wipe the freckles off my nose.

'So, how's it all going?' she asks, and I'm surprised to see how serious she looks.

I beam back at her. 'It's brilliant. I absolutely love being in the play.'

She smiles at my enthusiasm, but she still looks worried. 'And how are you coping with everything else – friends, schoolwork, that sort of thing? Are you managing to keep a good balance?'

I think about this for a second, wondering whether she could speak to Mr Chase about all the homework he keeps giving me. It really isn't fair of him when I'm so busy with all this other stuff.

'Actually,' I begin carefully, 'Mr Chase is giving us loads of homework. I thought that maybe …'

She stops me at once. 'When I gave you this part, I made it clear your schoolwork must come first. To be honest, I've been receiving complaints from several of your teachers, not just Mr Chase. I've been hearing about assignments handed in late, or not done properly, and about you dreaming in class and generally having rather a poor attitude. Several of your teachers tell me you're answering back rather a lot and not taking your classes seriously. What do you think?'

'I don't think that's fair,' I say at once. 'I don't think I've changed at all.'

She gives me a slight smile. 'Alright, but just think about what I've said.'

I turn and walk away without answering. I don't have to think about anything at all. I'm the most important person in the play, but that doesn't mean I've changed. It isn't my fault that Ashleigh's being so weird with me, and if anyone else has a problem with me that's just too bad. The best thing I can do is ignore them all and concentrate on being the most amazing Charlie Bucket anyone has ever seen.

Five

With only five weeks to go, we're rehearsing four times a week, and I'm exhausted. After hearing what my teachers have been saying about me, I try to work harder in class and on my assignments, just to keep everyone off my back. I seem to be spending most of my time at rehearsals or doing homework these days. I also spend hours practising by myself in front of the mirror. I have to be absolutely perfect as Charlie.

That will show everyone – Mum and Dad, Mr Chase, Ashleigh …

I stop myself right there. Whenever I find myself thinking about Ashleigh these days, I push the thought firmly back down. Some best friend she turned out to be – dropping me as soon as I got a star part. But it doesn't really matter because my new friends are much nicer than she is. Most of them are older than me, so I don't see them during lessons, but we have loads of fun at rehearsals. It's really cool hanging out with the year nine and ten girls. They're much more fun than the year sevens, who are *so* immature. Most of them don't even speak to me anymore because they're so jealous I'm the star.

The only bad thing about rehearsals is having to spend so much time with Rose. She's always there, and she's always completely silent. As far as I'm concerned, she's just wasting her time watching everything and making notes in her stupid notebook. I find it really easy to remember my lines and exactly where to stand, so I never need to write anything down.

Miss Ryner keeps suggesting that Rose and I meet in the evenings or at weekends to rehearse our lines. I always nod and smile, but whenever Rose suggests a time I make sure I'm busy. She eventually gets the message and stops asking.

She doesn't even look like Charlie. She's small, like me, but she has long, blonde hair, so she'd need a wig to play the part. Let's face it, I look much more like Charlie than she ever could, and I'm a far better actor. She's probably hoping she never has to go on stage and show everyone how awful she is. She must be terrified at the very thought.

Or maybe not. I'm talking to Grandpa Joe one afternoon, while we're waiting for the Oompa Loompas to finish a complicated dance, when there's a creaking sound behind us. Miss Ryner jumps across the stage and pushes me out of the way, just as the scenery behind me comes crashing down. I stare in horror at a large piece of wood, painted to look like the inside of Charlie's house.

Miss Ryner's face is very pale. 'That was close. Are you alright, Hannah?'

'I'm fine,' I say, rubbing my arm where she grabbed it. We both look at the space where the scenery was meant to be, but there's no one there.

Miss Ryner is clearly very shaken. 'What on earth happened? That piece of scenery was supposed to be fixed in place. We'll have to make sure it doesn't happen again, or we'll end up with you in hospital and Rose will have to go on instead of you.'

She laughs and turns towards the place where Rose always sits, silently taking notes, but for once she isn't there.

I overhear Miss Ryner having a word with some of the girls working backstage. She sounds quite angry as she insists that in future they must tie all the scenery to the rafters. With only two weeks to go we're rehearsing every day after school and using all the backdrops. The art class has done an amazing job, and it's much easier to act now that everything feels so real. There will be actual candy flowers for us to pick and eat during the performance. For now, we push pink and white marshmallows onto little green sticks and practise with those.

I walk up to Rose at the beginning of the next rehearsal. She's sitting quietly in her chair as usual and smiles when she sees me.

'Did you hear the scenery almost fell on me yesterday?' I ask in a casual voice.

She nods eagerly. 'Yes, wasn't that awful? Miss Ryner said it wasn't hooked on properly at the back.'

I give her a suspicious look. 'You seem to know an awful lot about it.'

She shrugs. 'I heard her talking to the stage manager. She said you could have been really hurt. I'm so glad you weren't.'

I pull enough of a face to show her I'm not convinced, but she doesn't seem to notice.

'I can't believe it's the dress rehearsal next Wednesday,' she says. 'Good luck, Hannah. Break a leg!'

I jump in shock, and she laughs. 'Don't worry – it's just what you say to people before a performance. It's a sort of anti-jinx to stop anything bad happening.'

I stare at her very hard without speaking then walk away with my mind racing.

I cycle home after Monday's rehearsal, feeling more exhausted than ever. Just as I reach the traffic lights, they turn red. I brake, but nothing happens, and I keep heading towards the main road. At the very last minute, I throw myself sideways off my bike, landing on the cycle path in a heap. I'm wearing shorts and I get a massive scrape along my thigh. It could have been worse, though, and I manage to push my bike the rest of the way home.

Mum opens the door and shrieks when she sees the blood on my leg.

'It's not too bad,' I tell her, leaning my bike against the wall and limping towards the house, 'but I've had time to think about it as I walked home. Someone cut my brake wires, and I almost went into the traffic.'

Scott wanders out and inspects my bike. 'No, they didn't. The brake wire's fine.'

He squeezes the brake handle then pokes at my back wheel. 'There's a twig stuck behind your brake pad. It must have slipped and jammed up the brakes when you tried to stop. Didn't you notice it when you started off?'

I shake my head. I was so tired after the rehearsal that I just jumped on my bike and started home. But even if the brake wires weren't cut, it seems very strange that a twig just happened to get stuck there. I suggest this to Mum, who doesn't look convinced.

'It happened to me the other day when I parked my bike under the trees,' she says. 'Luckily, I saw it before I started cycling home.'

I'm not at all convinced, but there's no point arguing. No one will believe me. I stump upstairs to take a bath, grumbling under my breath. 'Well, if you don't care that someone's trying to kill your only daughter, I can't make you. Just wait until I'm in hospital with all my bones broken. Maybe then you'll be sorry.'

Mum follows me upstairs. 'You don't really think this was done deliberately?' she asks. 'Why on earth would anyone do that?'

I shake my head without speaking. I'll never be able to prove anything. Rose is just like the Mafia. They're never there when bad things happen, but you absolutely know they were involved. Perhaps I need a bodyguard for the next couple of weeks. I'm the most important person in the school, and it looks as though someone doesn't like that. It isn't difficult to guess who that someone might be.

On Friday afternoon, we play softball as usual. This is usually one of my favourite lessons, but today my mind is full of thoughts of Rose. I'm wondering exactly how far she might go to make sure I don't get to play Charlie.

I'm standing at the plate, holding the bat loosely in my hands and thinking about this, when the ball whacks me in the mouth, and I yell in shock and pain. I don't even have to look up to see who was pitching. Rose is already running towards me with a look of fake horror on her face. I hold her off with one hand while I feel my teeth with the other. They all seem to be in place, but I've cut my lip. I can already feel it swelling.

'Lauren, get the ice pack!' calls Mr Bates. 'Are you alright, Hannah? That looks rather nasty. You need to keep your eye on the ball when you're playing softball. You looked as though you were half-asleep today. Are you tired?'

'Thyee did it on purpose!' I hiss as best I can through my swollen lip. 'Thyeez out to get me!'

'Who is?' He kneels down and hands me the ice pack. It feels good against my swollen lip.

'Wothze!' I hiss again. It's really annoying not being able to speak properly. I sound like a two-year old, and I can see some of the girls grinning at each other. I try again. 'Thyee wanth my part. Thyeeth trying to thpoil thingth for me.'

Mr Bates pulls me to my feet. 'That's enough of that. The only thing that happened is that you were half-asleep at the plate. You were lucky Rose was bowling so gently. But I do know you have rather a lot going on at the moment. Go and rest in the shade for a while with your ice pack.'

I open my mouth to protest, but he's already walking away. I sit at the very furthest edge of the field with the ice pack pressed to my mouth, sulkily watching the rest of the game. Ashleigh doesn't even come over to ask how I am. I've really had it with her. I wouldn't be friends with her again, even if she came and begged me – not that it looks as though she's going to.

By the end of the afternoon, my lip has returned to its right size, and all that's left is a sore place on my tongue where I bit it. Rose must be really fed up to think her latest attempt hasn't worked.

I count in my head – five more days to the dress rehearsal, and eight more days to the actual performance. Until then, I'll just have to watch myself every second of the day and stay far away from Rose. It's a battle of wits between us now, and I'm determined to do everything necessary to make sure she doesn't win.

Six

Aunty Jen arrives on our doorstep on Saturday morning, carrying a duffel bag. I zoom down the steps to meet her. 'Hi, Aunty Jen! Have you come to stay with us? Mum didn't say anything to me. What's in the bag?'

She gives me a hug. 'Not so many questions, young lady. Where's your mum?'

Mum appears at the front door, holding a bag just like Jen's. They smile at each other.

'All set?' asks Mum, and Jen nods.

I give Mum a suspicious look. 'All set for what? What's going on?'

Jen picks up both bags. 'I'm taking you away for the weekend, Hannah.'

I stare at her in disbelief. 'What are you talking about? I can't go anywhere this weekend. The play's next Saturday.'

I reach for my bag, but she holds it away from me. 'Do you have rehearsals this weekend?'

I shake my head.

'Do you know all your lines?' she asks.

I shrug. 'Yeah, I suppose.'

Of course, I do. I've known them for ages. But knowing my lines is one thing – forgetting them when I get on stage is quite another. That's what's been keeping me awake at night for the past few weeks.

'So, what's the problem? asks Aunty Jen, throwing our bags into the trunk of her car.

'Go on, love, you could do with a nice break,' says Mum.

She gives me a swift hug, and after a moment's thought I follow Jen to the car. This might not be such a bad idea, after all. Rose can't sabotage me if I'm not physically here. She won't have any idea where I've gone. I smile to myself at the thought of her walking around all the local streets looking for me.

Mum said this would a nice break for me, which probably means something really posh, like a hotel with a spa. After all, I'm a star now, and stars need pampering – everyone knows that. So, I hop into the car quite cheerfully and grin at Aunty Jen as we drive away.

We drive out of town and start driving towards the bush, which puzzles me a bit. Most of the spas are much closer in to Sydney. Maybe this is a special secret spa that only famous people know about and where they go just to get away from it all.

An hour later, we're way out in the bush and I've just about given up on the idea of a five-star hotel. I can't stand not knowing any longer, so I tap Aunty Jen's arm. 'Where are we going? It isn't Sydney, is it?'

It's as though she's read my mind because she gives me an amused smile. 'No, it isn't Sydney. I thought we should try to get away from all your fans and admirers this weekend and have a complete break from the bright lights.'

I wriggle uncomfortably. 'Don't be silly. I haven't got fans. It's just a school play.' As soon as I say this, I realise I don't mean it. It isn't just a school play. It's the most exciting thing that has ever happened to me.

'So, where are we going?' I ask again.

'Camping,' she says.

'Camping?' I echo.

She must hear the disappointment in my voice but she ignores it. 'Camping – miles from anywhere. Just you, me and the stars in the sky. It'll be great fun.'

I don't even bother to answer. It isn't my idea of a perfect weekend, but it looks as though I'm stuck with it.

We pull in at a tiny campsite at the bottom of a hill. There's a small stream running under some gum trees but not much else. There's a pile of blackened stones next to the stream where someone has built a fire at some time, but we seem to be the only ones here today.

'Where's the shower block?' I ask as I climb out of the car.

Aunty Jen raises an eyebrow and points towards the stream.

I pull a face. 'Toilets?'

She reaches into the car and hands me a small trowel.

I put my hands behind my back. 'Oh, yeuch, Aunty Jen!'

'Stop fussing,' she tells me. 'It'll be great.'

And, except for having to go behind a bush and dig a hole for a toilet, it actually is great. It's absolutely quiet on the campsite. There aren't any cars or people, and I feel myself relaxing for the first time in weeks. I didn't even bring my script with me, so I can't spend all my time reading it.

We spend the afternoon splashing around in the stream with a net, trying to catch yabbies. We don't catch any, but the water is lovely and cool in the afternoon heat.

As it goes dark, Aunty Jen shows me how to build a fire on the rocks near the water, well away from the trees. She's brought tins of stew to heat over the fire, and we eat it with chunks of crusty bread. We finish our meal and rinse out the pan in the stream before climbing into our sleeping bags. We rest on our elbows and roast huge marshmallows on twigs. They're fantastic – all smoky and crunchy on the outside and sweet and runny on the inside.

'How's the play going?' she asks through a mouthful of marshmallow.

I think about this for a moment. Whenever Mum asks me about the play, I say it's great, because I'm scared she'll say it's too much for me and I should pull out. But the performance is only a week away now, so I should be pretty safe.

'It's ok,' I say at last, spearing another fluffy marshmallow with my stick. 'It's hard work, of course.'

Aunty Jen gives me a sympathetic look. 'It must be. It was quite a lot to take on during your first year at high school.'

'I don't mind,' I say at once. 'I've always wanted to be an actor.'

She nods. 'Your Mum tells me you're good.'

I shrug. 'I suppose.'

'Is Ashleigh in the play too?' she asks.

I feel my face close up when she asks this. I roll over onto my other side so she can't see my expression. 'I'm not friends with Ashleigh anymore.'

'That's a shame,' she says mildly. 'You guys have always done everything together.'

'Yeah, well, things change,' I mutter.

'Because you're in high school, you mean?'

I struggle to find the right words. 'It isn't exactly that, but Ashleigh was really horrible to me when I got the part, and now she's gone off with Macy. They go horse riding together all the time.'

My voice cracks a bit, but Aunty Jen doesn't seem to notice. 'You probably haven't had much time for anything except the play this term,' she says.

At last, someone understands how tough it's been for me. I roll back to face her. 'Totally – but no one seems to care about that! I could have seen Ashleigh all the time once the play was over. She didn't have to go off with Macy.'

'You mean, she could have waited until you had time for her again?' asks Aunty Jen.

I feel my face turn red. 'I don't mean it like that, but this play is really important to me. Ashleigh ought to have known that, but she's really changed recently.'

'Maybe you've changed too?' she says gently.

I shake my head. 'I don't think I'm any different, just because I'm playing Charlie.'

She smiles at me. 'You don't think any of this has gone to your head, just a tiny bit?'

I stick out my lower lip. 'I can't help being the star, can I? It's a really important part, and they couldn't do the play without me, but that doesn't make me big-headed.'

'Of course not,' she agrees, 'but it might make everyone else feel as though you don't think they're quite as important as you.'

I don't answer, and she doesn't push me. I watch her dip a cup into the stream and pour the water onto the last embers of the fire. It sizzles and hisses and dies down, and we lie together in the warm darkness without speaking.

Jen's breathing gradually becomes slower and deeper, but I can't sleep. I'm remembering the hundreds of times Ashleigh and I have camped out together in her garden, giggling and talking for half the night. In year six, our class went camping for two nights, and Ashleigh and I shared a tent. We talked for hours about high school and how great it was going to be and how we'd go on to college together after that.

It doesn't look as though any of that will happen now, and a tear trickles down my cheek as I think of everything I've lost. For the first time, losing my best friend seems a really high price to pay just to be in a stupid school production. I have to talk to Ashleigh when I get home and make one last effort to put things right. I have a horrible feeling it might be too late, but I'm not giving up without a fight.

As soon as I've decided this, I roll over and star
to relax. I stare up at the stars, listening to the
stream gurgling along beside my head. When I finally
fall asleep, I sleep much better than I've done for
many weeks.

Seven

We arrive back home on Sunday evening, and I hug Aunty Jen goodbye. 'Thanks a lot, Aunty J. Let's do it again sometime.'

'Love you, Hannah,' she tells me. 'I'll see you on Saturday night for the big performance.'

I'd almost forgotten about the play, which is surprising as I've thought about nothing else for the past few months. Now that she's reminded me, I feel a bit sick.

Aunty Jen sees my expression and laughs. 'You'll be fine. You're the star!'

'I don't feel like a star,' I tell her quietly. It's the first time I've admitted this to anyone. People seem to think I'm not nervous – that I can handle it all – so that's how I try to behave.

She hugs me again. 'You'll always be my star. You always have been. I thought you knew that?'

I shake my head, and she smiles at me. 'Well, now you know. Anyway, I'll see you on stage on Saturday night. Are you going in to call Ashleigh now?'

I jump slightly. 'How did you know?'

'Just a hunch,' she says with a grin.

I turn and race through the front door. Mum's in the kitchen, cooking dinner, and I throw my bag towards her and snatch up the phone. 'Can't talk now. I'm calling Ashleigh!'

'About time, too!' she calls, as I disappear upstairs to my bedroom.

I sit on my bed and take a deep breath. My stomach is whirling around so fast that I feel sick. I dial Ashleigh's home number, and her mum answers.

'Hello, Hannah,' she says when she hears my voice. 'I haven't heard from you in a while.'

It seems like years before Ashleigh comes to the phone, and I feel a thrill of excitement when I finally hear her voice. Everything's going to be ok now. She and I will be best friends again, and it will be as though this past term never happened. She'll stop seeing that awful Macy, and we can hang out together, just as we used to.

'What do you want, Hannah?' asks Ashleigh, and my stomach gives a great jolt. She's never spoken so coldly to me before.

I jump in quickly, wanting to make her understand that everything's changed, and we can be best friends again. 'I wanted to ask you to the play.'

This isn't what I'd planned to say, but it's as good as anything, and I'm sure I can get her a ticket.

There's a long pause. 'I already have tickets to the play,' she says at last. 'I'm going with Macy and her Mum.'

'But I can get you front row seats,' I tell her. I'm pretty sure I'll be able to. No one will dare refuse the star anything she wants.

'That's fine, thanks,' she says. 'We already have seats.'

'Why Macy?' I ask.

Ashleigh's voice freezes. 'I like her, ok?'

This isn't going to plan, so I decide to move away from the subject of Macy. I clear my throat. 'Anyway, I just wanted to let you know I'll be able to see you lots as soon as the play's over. I'll have time for you again.'

'Right,' she says, her voice sounding flat. 'Well, I have to go now, Hannah. Bye.'

I stare at the phone for a long time. That didn't go right. I'll just have to try again. I'll call her as soon Wednesday's dress rehearsal is over. I'm not giving up without a fight.

By Wednesday afternoon, I'm feeling really nervous, even though it's only the dress rehearsal.

'Don't worry, Hannah,' Miss Ryner tells me when I arrive. 'Everything always goes wrong at dress rehearsals. It's good luck. It means that everything will go well on the night.'

She's right. Lots of things go wrong. The scene changers get muddled up and put the Buckets' house on stage when we're all meant to be in the chocolate factory. One of the Oompa Loompas gets so excited during the first dance that she slips and knocks a giant candy cane off the stage, smashing it into tiny pieces. Even worse, the girl playing Mrs Bucket keeps forgetting her lines, and Miss Ryner gets really upset with her.

I don't forget any of my own lines, and I manage to get through the whole performance, but I'm not acting as well as usual. I feel as though I'm walking through fog during the second half of the play, and I'm glad when it's finally over.

'It's fine, Hannah,' says Miss Ryner, noticing my downcast face. 'You seemed a little tired today, but you know your lines perfectly. As soon as the audience is here, you'll sparkle as much as you always do. Just concentrate on getting plenty of rest between now and Saturday.'

I nod and pick up my bag. She's probably right, but I don't feel very sparkly at all. As I turn to leave, I notice Rose staring at me, and I glare back at her. Maybe I wasn't at my best tonight, but I was still one hundred times better than she could ever be.

'Are you alright, Hannah?' she asks with a look of fake concern.

'What do you care?' I say and walk off before she can say anything else.

Even when I get into bed that night, I can't rest. I'm desperately tired, but I feel too hot to sleep. Everything is buzzing around in my head, which has started to ache. Sometime after midnight, I slip out of bed and creep quietly down to the kitchen to get myself a drink. I'm just sneaking the fridge door open to see whether Scott has left any of Mum's homemade lemonade when the kitchen door opens. I jump and let out a startled squeak.

'It's only me,' says Mum's voice.

She doesn't look cross, so I relax. 'I just wanted a drink,' I tell her.

'Chocolate milk?' she asks, and I nod.

She pours out two glasses, and we sit at the table together. I kick my foot against the table leg as I sip my chocolate milk. It slips gently across my throat, and I start to feel cooler.

'How was the dress rehearsal?' asks Mum. 'You didn't say much when you came in.'

I shrug. 'It was alright, I suppose. I didn't forget my lines, but I just felt so tired all the way through.'

She ruffles my hair. 'Well, that's very natural. You've had a pretty intense term, what with your schoolwork and all the rehearsals, and you haven't really had anyone to share it with, have you?'

By anyone, I know she means Ashleigh. I don't answer for a moment. I can't explain how important the play seemed to be, until I realised how much I'd lost.

'I have you,' I say at last, and she smiles.

'Of course you have, and you always will, but it isn't quite the same, is it?'

'No,' I agree, slurping down the last dregs of milk. I don't mean to say anything else, but Mum's face is so kind and understanding that I decide it might help to tell her after all.

'It's awful!' I burst out. 'Ashleigh dumped me as soon as I got the part. I could never find her at school, and then she hooked up with that horrible Macy. I've tried to talk to her, but she won't. All she talks about is Macy's stupid horses. She doesn't sit with me in maths now, so I don't have anyone to help me, and the rest of my class doesn't like me anymore, so I only have the older girls to talk to. I called Ashleigh on Sunday night after camping and told her we can be friends again as soon as I have more time, but she just hung up on me. I hate her!'

I finish in a great burst of tears, and Mum leans over to hug me. It feels so good. I've been feeling completely on my own for weeks now.

She holds me close until I finish sobbing. 'Why didn't you tell me any of this?'

'I thought you'd say I couldn't be Charlie,' I hiccup.

'I wouldn't have said that, but I might have been able to help you find a way to keep some balance in your life.'

I wipe my eyes. 'All the stuff I thought was really important turned out not to be, but by the time I found that out it was too late. I've lost my best friend.'

Mum stands and picks up our empty glasses. 'Not necessarily. I want you to go to bed and get some sleep now. I'll ring the school tomorrow morning and tell them you'll be coming in late. Let's just get Saturday over and done with, and then we can figure out how to make things right with Ashleigh.'

Eight

But I won't be able to talk to Ashleigh any time soon. I wake the following morning with a horrible sore throat. I try to swallow, but it feels as though I'm drinking fire. My throat burns, and when I sit up I start to sweat. I try to call Mum, but my voice won't come out. In the end, I bang my fist on the wall behind my head.

Mum comes in a minute later, carrying a tray She beams at me. 'You're awake at last! It's already eleven o'clock. You must have had a really good sleep I've made you some toast and tea. Don't worry, I've phoned the school and told them you won't be in unti this afternoon.'

I silently shake my head, and she looks at me more closely. 'You didn't sleep well?'

I shake my head again and point to my throat Mum puts the tray down and comes over to the bed.

'Tip your head back, and say *Aaaah*,' she says.

I open my mouth obediently, but I can't even manage an *Aaaah*.

She peers down my throat and feels my forehead. She shakes her head. 'Your throat is bright red, and you have quite a temperature. I'll get the thermometer, and then I'll phone the doctor.'

She disappears before I can stop her, and I sink back onto my pillow, thinking hard. The falling piece of scenery, the twigs in the bike brakes, the carelessly flung softball that just *happened* to split my lip. It's all coming together now. I was right to be suspicious. Rose failed to sabotage me all those other times, but she's finally succeeded. She's poisoned me with something untraceable, and now I can't speak.

When Mum comes back in, I wave at her frantically and mime writing.

'Paper and pen?' she asks. 'That's a good idea.'

She disappears again, returning a minute later with a large notebook and a biro. I scribble furiously – *This isn't just a sore throat. My understudy is trying to kill me.*

I look at this for a moment before crossing out the word *kill* and changing it to *hurt.*

I push it over to Mum, who reads it with an odd expression on her face. 'Excuse me?' she says.

I scribble again at top speed – *She's called Rose and she tried to make me fall off my bike and she pushed the scenery on top of me and threw a ball in*

75

my face. Now she's managed to poison me so I can't speak.

Mum bursts out laughing when she reads this. 'Really? A top-secret poison she managed to slip into your food, perhaps? She sounds like a very smart girl.'

I glare at her and grab the pen again – *I saw her at dress rehearsal yesterday. She probably did it then.*

'How?' asks Mum.

Water fountain, maybe? I write, although even I can see how lame that looks.

Tears prickle my eyes. First, I'm in danger of being too ill to act on Saturday, and now my own mother is making fun of me.

Mum pats my shoulder. 'I'll bring Dr Mason in to see you when he arrives.'

I lie there, staring out of the window. My head hurts, my throat is on fire and my best friend hates me. I've never been so miserable in my life.

Eventually, I hear Dr Mason's car on the drive. He follows Mum into the bedroom and smiles down at me. 'So, young lady, I hear you're being poisoned by an assassin. Open your mouth, and I'll take a look.'

I glare at Mum and turn my head away. Dr Mason pats my arm. 'I'm only joking, Hannah. Open up, and we'll see what's going on.'

He shines a light down my throat and quickly swabs it. I choke, cough and glare at him again.

'Sorry about that,' he says, pushing his thermometer into my ear. He takes it out and looks at it. 'Thirty-nine! That's not so good. Now, I'm going to drip a little bit of this liquid onto the swab and put it into this card. I suspect what you're actually suffering from is strep throat, rather than poisoning, but let's make sure. And there it is …'

He shows me the little line starting to appear in the window. 'Just as I thought – strep throat. I'll get you started on antibiotics right away and prescribe you some painkillers. You'll be feeling much better by tomorrow, and you'll probably be able to go back to school on Monday.'

Monday? I can't believe he just said that. I frantically write a question in my notebook and wave it at him.

He peers at the paper. 'Saturday evening? Not a chance, I'm afraid. You'll barely have your voice back by then. You'll probably be well enough to go and watch but performing is out of the question. Do they have someone who can go on for you?'

Mum sees my face and waves at him to follow her out of the room. As the door closes behind them, I hear her voice murmuring, '… the lead part. It's all she thinks about.'

I hear his sympathetic voice but not what he answers.

I lie with my face pushed into the pillow, crying until I'm completely out of tears. When Mum brings me a cold drink and my antibiotics, I turn away and refuse to look at her.

She sits on the edge of the bed and strokes my hair. 'I'm so sorry, Hannah. Here, swallow these. Can I get you anything else?'

I shake my head then pick up the pen and scribble so hard that it tears the paper – *I don't care what he says. I'm going anyway.*

I roll over and start to climb out of bed, but my legs give way at once. If Mum hadn't been there to catch me, I'd have fallen over.

'I'm so sorry,' she says again, helping me back into bed and tucking the quilt around me.

I hate you! I scribble and close my eyes.

'No, you don't,' she says gently.

I hear the bedroom door click shut behind her. I keep my eyes squeezed tight shut as the truth sweeps over me. I'm really not going to get well in time. I'm not going to be in the play. All my hard work, the long hours of practise and losing Ashleigh has been for nothing. Rose Simms will be the star after all Everyone will be applauding her and saying how brilliant she is. I just can't bear it.

It gets worse. I'm still in bed on Friday afternoon, although Mum says I can get up for a while this evening. I hear the doorbell ring, and a moment later Mum puts her head round the door 'Visitor for you, Hannah.'

I sit up at once. It's Ashleigh! She's heard how sick I am, and she wants to be friends again. I smooth my tangled hair and look expectantly towards the door, only to see Rose standing there, clutching a large bunch of grapes.

'What do *you* want?' My voice has come back enough for me to hiss, which is quite useful right now.

Rose sits on the end of my bed and hands me the grapes. 'I came to say how sorry I am that you're ill I honestly didn't want to be Charlie instead of you.'

'Sure, you did,' I croak, curling my lip as scornfully as possible. Maybe she didn't actually poison me, but I bet she would have done, given half the chance.

Rose speaks more firmly than usual, looking me straight in the eye. 'No, I didn't. I know you don't like me, Hannah, although I don't really know why. I think you're brilliant as Charlie, and it's horrible you're so ill. I wish it was me instead.'

Me too, I think, until I see her face. It's all pale and worried, and I suddenly realise she means what she says. She didn't want to take my part. I've been so wrapped up in myself this term that I've got everything else out of proportion. None of this is her fault. Even I know that.

'It's ok,' I whisper. 'I don't really think you poisoned me. The doctor says it's strep throat. It's just bad timing.'

'Thanks.' She looks relieved.

I decide to be honest with her. I have nothing left to lose now, except for a bit of pride.

I take a deep breath. 'I didn't mean to be so horrible to you, Rose. I just started thinking I was a bit more important than I really was. Miss Ryner was right. It's lucky I have an understudy, or no one would be able to do the play.'

'It won't be nearly as good without you,' she says sadly.

I give her a half smile. 'Yes, it will. It'll be just as good. You know all the lines perfectly, and you'll be great.'

We talk for a while longer, until I can't hiss anymore. She tells me how much she hated moving to our town and not knowing anyone. Although she doesn't actually say it, I know I've made things worse by being so horrible to her at rehearsals. I tell her a bit about me and Ashley, and she sympathises. To tell the truth, by the time she gets up to leave I'm feeling pretty small. It's no wonder that hardly anyone likes me anymore.

'Good luck,' I whisper as she leaves. 'Break both your legs.'

She smiles back. 'Will you be coming tomorrow night?'

I hesitate. 'I'm not sure. Probably not.'

'I understand,' she says quietly. 'See you.'

She disappears, and I wonder whether Mum will come in and say, 'I told you so.' She doesn't, of course. She isn't like that. She appears in my doorway an hour later, looking pleased.

'I have a message for you, Hannah. Ashleigh phoned earlier and said she was very sorry to hear you've been so ill. Macy's mum can't go to the play after all, and she wondered whether you might like the extra ticket.'

I shake my head violently. 'I can't!'

'*Can't?*' says Mum. 'That isn't a word we hear very often from Hannah Davies. Just think about it.'

And before I can answer, she disappears.

Nine

By Saturday morning, I still haven't made up my mind. It would be awful to watch someone else play my part. Having to clap and cheer would be even worse. But it isn't really my part, is it? Rose will be great, and everyone will enjoy the play, and that's all that really matters.

I stay in bed until lunchtime then take a shower and wash my hair. If I'm going to do this, I'm determined to look my best.

Aunty Jen appears mid-afternoon with a bag of my favourite toffees. My throat hardly hurts at all now, so we sit in the garden and eat them while we watch Scott cut the grass.

'I'm so proud of you, Hannah,' she tells me.

'I'm not,' I say honestly. 'I've been a bit of a pain. It's no wonder everyone thinks I've got too big for my boots.'

She laughs. 'There have been times in your life when I've thought no boots could be big enough for you, but this isn't one of them. Your Mum called me this morning and told me you've decided to go tonight. You're one in a million, Hannah. Do you know that?'

I'm really embarrassed when she says this, but it's nice to know not everyone thinks I'm a complete loser. When she finally stands up to leave, she gives me a huge hug. 'See you tonight. I hear you're sitting with Ashleigh.'

'And Macy,' I say gloomily.

She smiles. 'It's a start.'

She's right – it *is* a start, so after an early dinner I dress in my favourite cropped jeans and blue striped top. When we arrive at school, I start to open my car door then freeze.

'I can't do this!' I say, panic-stricken.

'Nonsense!' says Mum firmly. 'I haven't yet seen the thing you couldn't do if you put your mind to it.'

'What if she doesn't want to speak to me?' I ask, my voice wobbling slightly.

Mum smiles. 'She saved you a seat, didn't she?'

'What if everyone thinks it serves me right for being so stuck up?'

She smiles again. 'That's their problem. Haven't they ever made mistakes? At least you have the guts to face yours.'

That's the worst thing about mothers. They're usually right.

'Ok, here I go!' I breathe deeply and start off across the car park to the main entrance.

'Good luck!' Mum calls after me. 'Remember, Hannah, this is the performance of a lifetime for you. You aren't going to let everyone see how upset you are and spoil things for Rose. Put your chin up, and let's see just what kind of an actress Hannah Davies really is.'

I walk into the hall and make my way slowly towards the fifth row, where Ashleigh and Macy are already sitting. This is more nerve-racking than walking onto the stage as Charlie Bucket. I feel as though everyone in the hall is staring at me, some of them sympathising but most of them thinking I've got what I deserved for being so proud about my star part. I keep my head high and squeeze my hand hard around the bunch of flowers I've brought to give Rose after the play.

Ashleigh turns her head when I appear and gives me a small smile.

'Hi,' I say, sitting down next to her.

Macy is sitting on Ashleigh's other side. She smiles at me too. 'Hi, Hannah.'

Ashleigh's face is completely unreadable, and I know it's up to me to speak first. After all, she made the first move by calling to offer me the seat.

'I've been a jerk!' I say in a rush.

Ashleigh nods. 'Yup.'

I feel my face turning pink. 'I know I have. I've been a complete idiot all term.'

'How much of an idiot?' she asks.

I feel a rush of relief when I see she's hiding a grin. I've known her far too long not to be able to read her face. I think about this carefully.

'An idiot times six to the power of twenty,' I say at last, 'although I don't know exactly how much that is now you won't help me with my maths anymore.'

Ashleigh is grinning properly now. 'It's quite a lot, actually. It's enough.'

I breathe more easily and relax back into my chair.

'I'm really sorry you've been so ill,' she says, and I can see she means it.

'It's actually ok,' I tell her. 'I was really upset at first, but then I realised I was even more upset about the two of us not being friends anymore.'

'It was my fault too,' she says, staring down at her feet. 'I *did* feel a bit jealous when you got the star part. I just needed some time by myself, but by the time I was fine with it all, you were hanging out with the older girls and thinking you were really special, so I didn't bother.'

'I wish you had,' I say quietly.

She squeezes my hand. 'I wish I had too.'

I give a sigh of relief. Everything's alright. We still understand each other. Maybe we haven't lost everything, after all.

'Would you like some chocolate, Hannah?' asks Macy, breaking me off a piece.

'Thanks,' I say, cramming it into my mouth.

'Sorry about the throat,' she adds.

'Thanks,' I say again.

'Ashleigh suggested you might like to come riding with us some time,' she says. 'There's a pony in the field where I keep my horse. She's really calm, and she never throws anyone off.'

'That sounds good, thanks,' I say with my mouth full of chocolate.

To be honest, I'd sort of thought that once Ashleigh and I were friends again, she wouldn't want to hang out with Macy anymore. But this could work too. We can probably both still have other friends and still be Ash and Hannah, just as we always were.

'Everyone in our year hates me,' I tell Ashleigh as casually as possible. I don't want to show how upset I am that hardly anyone is speaking to me.

'They'll get over it,' she says calmly.

'I doubt it,' I say. 'They all think I'm a real show off.'

'Do you blame them?' she asks.

I think about this for a moment. 'No, but I really wish I could have this term all over again. I'd do everything differently.'

'You're here to support Rose, aren't you?' she asks. 'You didn't have to come tonight. Most people will think that's pretty cool.'

'I saw Rose,' I say. 'She came to see me yesterday.'

Ashleigh laughs. 'That was extremely brave of her. Did you bite her head off?'

'No,' I say with as much dignity as I can manage. 'She's actually quite nice. I don't know whether you've realised that.'

'I have,' she says.

'Well, I think she's going to be amazing tonight. I've seen her rehearse, and I think she's going to surprise everybody.'

Ashley nods. 'Maybe I'll audition with you next year.'

'But you hate acting!' I say, surprised.

She shrugs. 'It might be fun to have just a small part. What do you think, Macy?'

Macy pretends to think about this very carefully. 'Perhaps they'll do Cinderella next year,' she says. 'If Rose is really as good as Hannah says, she can be Cinderella. You guys could be in it too.'

Ashleigh tries to look offended. 'As what, exactly?'

'Take a wild guess,' says Macy. 'You'd make brilliant ugly sisters.'

We're still snorting with laughter when the curtain begins to rise. As the lights go down and we see Rose sitting on the bed in her tumbledown house, Ashleigh squeezes my hand hard. I'm grateful that she understands I'm not totally ok with this. Of course, I'm not. I'm just mostly ok, and that will have to do for now. Anyway, there will be other plays, and if Ashleigh auditions with me next year it will be ten times as much fun, even if we don't get star parts. There's a sudden loud whistling sound a few rows behind us, and we start to giggle again. Gran must have switched on her hearing aid.

Rose is awesome. I knew she'd be fine, but she's way better than that. She seems to glow as she speaks her lines, and when the play ends everyone jumps to their feet. I can't cheer yet, but I clap with my hands over my head, just in case Rose can see me. Eventually, the applause dies down, and the lights go up. The three of us look at each other.

'I told Emily and Lauren I'd meet them afterwards,' says Macy. 'Catch you both later?'

She disappears into the crowd behind us, and I pick up the bunch of roses I brought with me. They're a bit squashed, but I pat them gently into place.

'I picked these for Rose,' I tell Ashleigh. 'They seemed appropriate. Come with me while I find her?'

'In case you get lost?' she asks, following me through the rows of chairs towards the corridor.

I shake my head. 'In case you do.'

She smiles at me. 'I'm not going anywhere.'

Me and Ash – Ash and me. Other friends may come and go, but some things will never change. She takes my arm, and we make our way through the chattering crowd to give Rose her flowers.

Thank you for reading this book. I do hope you enjoyed it. If you did, please consider leaving a review on Amazon. It helps new readers find my books, and I really appreciate it.

Also, please visit my website at rjwhittaker.com for news about upcoming books, free offers and competitions. If you have questions about Pom Pom or any of my other books, you can contact me directly via the website. I always love talking to readers and hearing their thoughts and suggestions.

About the Author

RJ Whittaker was born in the UK, but one day she got lost and now she lives a few miles away in Australia. She learned to read long before you did, so you probably have some catching up to do. If you like books as much as she does, you'll probably enjoy reading about a monkey called *Pom Pom*. He came to live with RJ's family several years ago and has caused so much trouble that RJ often thinks about running away to get some peace.

If monkeys aren't your thing – although they really should be – you'll probably enjoy RJ's books about people just like you. There's *Hannah Takes The Lead* – a story about a girl who lands her dream part in the school play but loses all her friends, and *Jasmine Moves In* – a story of bullying, cupcakes and sweet revenge.

To find out more about these books, and maybe even win yourself a free copy, just follow the trail of banana skins to my website at www.rjwhittaker.com.

Also by R J Whittaker

Jasmine Moves In

She's always wanted a neighbour her own age – but does it have to be this one?

Rosalie is delighted when Jasmine moves in next door, but it doesn't take her long to discover Jasmine isn't as perfect as she seems. However, no one believes her, not even her own family.

Rosalie realises she must find the courage to deal with her bully all by herself. But can she find a way, before she loses all her friends? She isn't exactly seeking revenge, but a little justice might be nice.

A relatable and amusing story about a girl dealing with friendships, family and high school bullies – discovering along the way the resilience she never knew she had.

Pom Pom The Great

A boy who needs a friend and a monkey who needs a home ...

When Pom Pom leaps through the bedroom window one night, he turns James' life upside down. Pom Pom tells everyone he's the tidiest, quietest, most helpful monkey anyone has ever met, and the family is lucky to have him.

There's just one small problem. James refuses to get rid of his badly behaved teddy bear, who quickly becomes Pom Pom's worst enemy. One of them has to go, and Pom Pom is determined it won't be him.

If James wants Pom Pom to stay, he has to promise to keep him out of trouble. What could possibly go wrong?

Pom Pom Moves House

Pom Pom's family is on the move, and there's plenty to do. It's lucky he's such a helpful monkey, always willing to lend a paw. The family would never get through it all without him. Pom Poms are the very best at moving house.

Pom Pom Starts School

School quickly becomes one of Pom Pom's very most favourite things. He can hardly wait to show his school report to Teddy. If that doesn't prove which one of them is the smartest, nothing will. Pom Poms are the very best at going to school.

Pom Pom The Pirate

After a successful term at school, it's time for Pom Pom's first summer holiday. He swims in the sea, disguises himself as an iceberg, battles a giant crab and discovers a treasure map. Pom Poms are the very best at summer holidays.

Pom Pom The Brave

When Pom Pom needs to have his tonsils out, he knows how much his family will miss him. He must get home as quickly as possible to look after them. Luckily, Pom Poms are the very best at having operations.

Pom Pom Helps Out

Mum's sister is having a baby, and Pom Pom and Mum go to Scotland to help out. While he's there, Pom Pom visits a castle, hunts for ghosts and tries to steal the crown jewels. He's also happy to help out when his new cousin arrives. Pom Poms are the very best at babies.

Made in United States
North Haven, CT
23 December 2022

30061420R00059